Labor Pains . . .

Waiting to push!

KOLLIN L. TAYLOR

authorHOUSE®

AuthorHouse™
1663 Liberty Drive
Bloomington, IN 47403
www.authorhouse.com
Phone: 1-800-839-8640

Published by AuthorHouse   12/23/2014

ISBN: 978-1-4969-6121-1 (sc)
ISBN: 978-1-4969-6120-4 (e)

Library of Congress Control Number: 2014922721

To those who have endured or are enduring a test of faith like Abraham, who waited twenty-five years for the LORD God to fulfill His promise to give him a son. Before you can push, you have to persevere.

Contents

Acknowledgments

Life has its share of challenges, so thank You, my Heavenly Father, for faithfully keeping Your promise to never leave or forsake us. You make the wait, and the labor pains, worth it.

Most of the time others will not be able to relate to what you are going through, but then someone comes along who can relate to you because they are going through something too. That person usually becomes a friend. For me, Kashawna was that friend who also received a promise from the LORD God that was unmistakable. However, the wait was more painful than the labor pains, because at least with labor pains it's only a matter of time before the push to delivery.

Sterlin King, thank you for your generosity.

Introduction

A woman carrying a child to term is a beautiful thing. But then it becomes uncomfortable, and the child eventually has to come out in order to grow and fulfill its potential. However, there is usually a period of painful contractions before an expectant mother's body is ready so she can give birth by pushing.

There are times in life when both women and men are "pregnant" with something inside that causes a great deal of pain, but they have to keep persevering until it is time to push and give birth to that dream, vision, thought, etc. *Labor Pains: Waiting to Push!* is about what we go through before giving birth to what the Lord placed inside of us.

Sea of Teal

The earth was covered in teal,
And tragedy fueled our zeal.
We gathered to celebrate life,
Because a man lost his mother and wife.

So, as long as the Lord gives us breath,
Let's celebrate life instead of death.
Please cast away your pain,
So the suffering won't be in vain.

United, let us stand,
As we walk hand in hand.

Inspired by the Vicki Welsh Fund's "Whisper Walk" for Ovarian
Cancer. For more information visit http://vickiwelshfund.org/

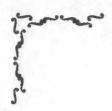

The Air

Sometimes it's like life's not fair.
I could feel it in the atmosphere.
The crowd was quite large,
And their pain gave the air an electric charge.

There's one thing I couldn't do at all,
And that was look at the photographs on the wall.
Many are still here with us today,
But the wall had those who passed away.

Inspired by the Vicki Welsh Fund's "Whisper Walk" for Ovarian Cancer. For more information visit http://vickiwelshfund.org/

New Lease

Tears streaming down her face,
Fitting in yet feeling out of place.
She has spent two years cancer-free.
Yet the day is going by painfully.
It's sometimes hard to celebrate the gift of life
When you're scarred by the strife.

Inspired by the Vicki Welsh Fund's "Whisper Walk" for Ovarian
Cancer. For more information visit http://vickiwelshfund.org/

Somber Pace

Even if this were a race,

We can't help but walk at a somber pace.

Every step gives our hearts a lift

And reminds us that life is a very precious and heavenly gift.

Inspired by the Vicki Welsh Fund's "Whisper Walk" for Ovarian Cancer. For more information visit http://vickiwelshfund.org/

The Circle

Everyone is a survivor today,
Even if they passed away.
The walk created an awesome scene,
As young and old blazed a trail that was serpentine.
You couldn't tell the beginning from the end,
As every stranger became a friend.

Inspired by the Vicki Welsh Fund's "Whisper Walk" for Ovarian Cancer. For more information visit http://vickiwelshfund.org/

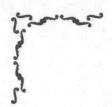

Warmth

We always learn so much along the way,
And it was no different today.
We sometimes see the world filled with cold, dark places.
But today there's only warmth on these faces.

Inspired by the Vicki Welsh Fund's "Whisper Walk" for Ovarian Cancer. For more information visit http://vickiwelshfund.org/

Life's Grip

Survivors wore a feathery boa on this trip.
It was very fitting because of a boa constrictor's grip.
When life's challenge may have caused you to pass away,
You keep holding on and fight for another day.

Inspired by the Vicki Welsh Fund's "Whisper Walk" for Ovarian Cancer. For more information visit http://vickiwelshfund.org/

The Walk

On the field is a Zumba dancer,
While on the track they walk against cancer.
Thousands join in the fight
Against cancer by walking all night.

The "race" is not just based on distance.
The goal is to eradicate cancer, this instance.
They lined the track with the names of those who passed away.
But we walked for life today.

Those on the sidelines support with cheers,
But for my late aunt Carole I feel the tears.
Cancer comes in a wide variety,
So thanks to charities like the American Cancer Society.

Matthew 6

You achieve a greater level of clarity
When you give something to charity.
Funds keep them going strong.
But if you believe money is the most desired gift, you're wrong.

So, if you feel as if you've lost your way,
Give something to a charity today.
But before you get into the charitable mix,
Take the advice in Matthew 6.

Spark

When iron sharpens iron, it doesn't require sharp edges.
Even blunt edges will sharpen the ledges.
Heed the words of the wise,
But be leery of the words of those who are only wise in their own eyes.
Don't discount the words of those whose elevator seemingly doesn't
go to the top,
Because you can learn things wherever the elevator makes a stop.

Two blunt stones and your desire
Can cause a spark that creates a fire.
One simple spark gives you a lot to learn,
And the same spark can cause an entire forest to burn.

Nature

Volcanoes are not easily cooled.

But we're humans, and sometimes we're easily fooled.

Such is the nature of the beast.

The predator stalks its prey and pounces before its gluttonous feast.

However, whether a predator or a prey,

Everything will have its day.

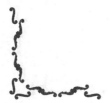

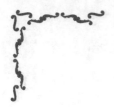

The Biological Clock Rock

Tick! Tock!
Such is the sound of my biological clock.
TICK! TOCK!
The sounds cause my body to rock.

But as the clock causes my body to quake,
I can't make a hormonal mistake.
A child is a gift for life,
And I can't choose a man who wouldn't choose me as a wife.
So I'll have to hit the snooze alarm,
Because impatience now would do future harm.

No Me, without You

Sometimes I have horrible days.
But can you imagine the oceans without waves?
Sometimes it seems as if life's challenges won't stop.
But what would a valley be without a mountaintop?

In many ways this is very true:
There would be no me without You.

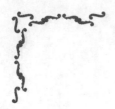

New Page

I remember how I hoped and prayed;
I tearfully wished you had stayed.
I wondered what could've torn us apart
And left a void in my heart.
Our life was filled with glory
Until you changed the story.

You didn't give me a thought or look
Because someone else was filling your book.
But now I don't feel any rage
For holding on to your page.
Because when I pray,
I thank the Lord for taking you away.

Now that I've ranted,

Please stop taking God's precious gift of love for granted.

And here's one thing more:

Don't treat sharing love like a chore.

But our story still has one more paragraph,

Because the LORD God will get the last laugh.

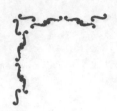

Part II

Every time I blow a fuse and vent,
I have to turn around and repent.
This thorn in my side makes me weak,
And death or relief is what I seek.

The depths of my pain made me pray
And ask God for death rather than face another day.
The Lord knows the story, and I only have a clue
That it hurts worse when the same thing happens in Part II.

But I woke up to another day of grief.
I didn't die and there's still no relief.
Why is this my price to pay?
Why do I have to live like this another day?

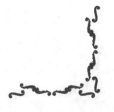

To rebel is to fight a battle I can't win,
And to express the depths of my pain is a sin.
Times like this make me feel hated.
I'm grateful for life but despise I was ever created.

Lord, it's obvious that I'm in distress.
I'm impatiently waiting … for You to rescue me from this mess.
My Lord, I know You can hear, see, and feel my grief.
Yet You withhold my relief.

This feels like such a calamity,
A test of my faith, patience, and humanity.
But if You had let me go through this with dignity,
I would not have learned so much about humility.

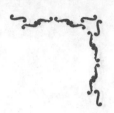

Bigger Fish

So many of God's servants asked Him to let them die.

But the Lord refused, because He had bigger fish to fry.

Sometimes the struggles made them feel so defeated.

But the Lord is on the throne, and He won't be unseated.

It's hard to continue when the whole world's against you.

However, just keep on doing what He wants you to do.

When the pressures stress your last nerve,

Remember, it's God and not man that you serve.

Shared Fact

Battered and buried under a pile of rubble.
Then you finally said, "Here comes trouble!"
It's so much harder to react
When you're warned after the fact.

All this time I thought you cared,
Until I found what you knew wasn't shared.
It's so much harder to react
When you're warned after the fact.

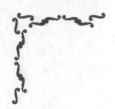

Not by Sight

Faith is not based on what we can see.
It is trusting in the Lord for what will be.
It's putting our anxieties to rest
And letting Him do what He does best.

Adversity is a time when God is sometimes hated.
But don't forget: He's the Creator, and we were created.
So before you shower Him with abuse,
Remember the potter made some pots for special use.
We are His pots crafted from clay
That He gives and He also takes away.

Being a child of the Almighty God
Won't spare us from His disciplinary rod.
Here's one more thing we can't afford to forget:
Having faith doesn't mean we'll enjoy what we get.

Conflict Resolution

Sometimes the conflict is internalized, and nothing is ever said.
One person has the discussion, entirely in their head.
The relationship suffers from pollution,
Because only one person has the problem, and the solution.
And instead of working toward a mutual goal,
One person is left with a lap full of burning coal.
Unfortunately, sometimes that's the very first clue
That your partner has been battling with you.
You get hit with a left and a right
Before you even knew you were in a fight.

It's hard for a couple to be in one accord
When the relationship was not ordained by the Lord.

Dear Friend

I can imagine how you're feeling,
And I know how much you desire healing.
I know you miss your heavenly gift
And that your soul could use a lift.

It's like the parable of the lost sheep,
As the one you miss makes you weep.
Happily ever was anticipated,
But now you may feel like your love was wasted.

I know what it's like to pray
And say, "Please Lord, end my pain today …"
Only to close the day and cry,
As you wonder, "Lord, why?"
If they only had a clue
About the pain of loving someone who doesn't love you.

Your heart flutters like the wings of a dove
As it overflows with precious love.
But, like heated snow,
Your love melts and starts to flow.
And even if the Lord tells you to let go,
Your heart keeps saying no.

It's no surprise that your greatest fear
Is that you'll never get to have your love near.
But to you, my dear friend,
This is the beginning, not the end.
You hurt, and there's no pretending!
But there's still hope for a very happy ending.

We will reap what we sow,
And time spent apart is time to grow.
When the Lord pulls people apart,
It hurts as emotions tug at the heart.

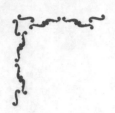

But the Lord is very clever,
And He knew that love wouldn't last forever.
So, He reserved a later date
For you to experience a love that's truly great.
Trust in Him that patience pays
And He hears the one who prays.
He'll wipe away those tears
And replace them with blessed cheers.

So until He blesses you with your dear,
I'm the friend He sent until your love gets here.
I'm also here to remind
You that your love is being skillfully refined.
In time you'll share stories about the lessons learned,
And you'll forget the days of feeling spurned.

You may feel down and dejected,
But even some cornerstones were once rejected.
The words from my heart are still flowing, but I'll stop
By reminding you that the crème always rises to the top.

To some it may seem like lip service or I'm insane
When I say, "I can feel your pain."
The pain that you feel is unique to you,
But the pain I feel gives me a clue.

Things may not feel as if they are going your way,
So I pray hope finds you every day.

Ill Prepared

You are everything I want my beloved to be.
But it's too bad you're not "ready" for me.
A chance at love doesn't require that you're prepared.
But a love like this can make even the fearless scared.
Sometimes, love is a rude awakening, versus a pleasant surprise,
And it never goes away, no matter how hard one tries.

For so many this is a very special time of year,
And I hope they'll have a special love near.
I hope what they find is the real thing,
Because there are fake trees to go with a holiday fling.

We can get ready for things like rain from above,
But we never have to get ready for love.
A love like this is something everyone can see.
But only you would have gotten every part of me.

Single Wife and Mother

I can imagine how you feel.
A single married mom is a paradox that's real.
Oh, there's one more title on your shoulder!
You serve your country as a soldier.

You're a mother every day and night,
But on weekends you engage in another fight.
Life's good but to make ends meet
Your husband works hard on his feet.

You show your family tender love and care,
And it hurts when you leave for training every year.
This is one of the reasons why I say,
"Treat every day like it's Mother's Day."

As Prescribed

The pain couldn't be described.
But the meds were prescribed.
I really didn't care
That they were left over from last year.
What were they going to do to me,
Because they were prescribed legally?
I wasn't going to pour them down the drain,
Because the bottle said, "Take as needed for pain."

Restless Itch

When someone wants to leave, don't say no.
Just open the door and let them go.
What happens next may make you weep,
Because the devil tries to remove things the Lord meant for you to keep.

The Lord will join you, so you can be happy,
But the devil plants seeds that make one of you think things are crappy.
God will bless you richly, but the devil tries to make you feel poor
And walk away because you can't take it anymore.

God will bless you with a love that makes you rich,
While the devil distracts with a restless itch.
The devil can make you feel trapped in a relationship that actually
sets you free.
But don't forget that it won't be easy, even when it was meant to be.

So, when someone asks you to leave, don't say no.
They'll remember your warmth if they end up freezing in the snow.

Dr. Time

This visit won't require a proctor.
And it's never late, because time is your doctor.
Dr. Time doesn't know how you feel,
But it provides the medicine for you to heal.

Experiencing pain never feels great,
And neither does it when Dr. Time says, "Please wait."
But here's what Dr. Time eventually reveals:
It may be the doctor, but it's God's love that truly heals.

It's highly contagious, but Dr. Time won't wear a glove,
Because time is here to spread God's love.

Ill Effects

The high of a thrill
May result in a big spill.
Just like how getting seriously ill
Will result in a large hospital bill,
And you can't rest assured,
Even if you're among the insured.

The recommended daily allowance of vitamin C
Will not prevent a medical emergency.
It takes more than a crash cart
To stop a bleeding heart.
And how do you clear an infected lung
When you're drowning in life's dung?

Golden

It's disheartening to find out that someone you dated
Was not golden; he or she was gold-plated.
Because when you drill down into their core,
The golden crust covers a rusty iron ore.

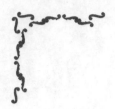

I See

This felt so great when it was a thought,
But look at what reality brought.
Now that the luster has faded,
I'm left feeling so jaded.
How can this be?
Why was the upside all I could see?
A decision that felt so right
Is now filled with regret when illuminated by hindsight.

Sportscaster

My life has run amuck.
I've been slapped around like a hockey puck.
I feel like I've lost it all,
After being bounced around like a basketball.

I am blessed, but I still grumble
With the force of a downhill skier that takes a tumble.
I'm not a loser, even when I end up in the losers' bracket,
Like a ball that's been whacked by a tennis racket.

All my attempts to float sky-high
Were restrained like a pelota in jai alai.

My Appeal

My dear Lord, I file this appeal
With respect and loving zeal.
You know I have been ripped apart
And that these words come straight from my heart.

I solely depend on You,
Because I need You to get me through.
I won't complain and say I've had more than I can take,
Because You can fix me regardless of the depth of the break.
My life is better than living in jail,
But it makes me feel like I consistently fail.

Please, dear Lord, let me know what I need to do.
Am I being punished for disappointing You?
It has been a while since my repentance,
And this feels like an extended sentence.

Is the reason for my pain,
Because You view me with disdain?
Everything I'm going through
Sometimes makes me wonder if I'm loved by You.

For some, those words were probably not anticipated.
But it is written, Jacob You loved, but Esau You hated.
You know it intensifies my plight
When I see blessings missing me to my left and right.

Everyone gets wet when they stand out in the rain,
But sometimes I feel like I'm the only one getting showered with pain.
So, my dear Lord, is there something I'm failing to do?
Only You can give me a breakthrough.

Gladiator

A stadium filled with haters,
And I'm on a field with gladiators.
Bodies covered in armor that the noisy crowd causes to rattle.
Blood seeping from veins starving for oxygen needed to battle.
Swords, chains, whips, and shields.
But victory is not determined by what a man wields.
I'm exhausted and searching for my next breath.
What some view as a sport is actually a matter of life and death.

Faithful Curiosity

A broken heart on the mend.

My dear Lord, when will You bring this to an end?

You didn't promise me happily ever after.

But You promised me someone special to share days filled with love and laughter.

And as we give You all the praise,

Please don't forget the children You said we would raise.

I have faith in You even though when I look around to see,

There's no one else here, no one but me.

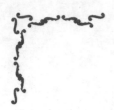

Now

Today is filled with sorrow
Because you won't be here tomorrow.
You will not have a clue
Of how much I will miss you.
My heart and soul will forever pay
For what I didn't do or say.
Your passing will somehow
Remind me to focus on the now.
A relationship will always be hollow
When we miss today by focusing on tomorrow.
If I could only have one more try
To say, "I love you," before saying good-bye.

Temp

It is hard to be bold
When the temperature is ice cold.
However, everyone feels beat
When God turns up the heat.

Bright Side

We all have more problems than the world can see.

But I don't want your problems, so I'll keep my own and be happy being me.

When stressed I sometimes wish I were a bird, so that I could be free.

But when it's raining, the bird may wish that it were me.

I've never liked being in weather that's freezing cold,

But I know that the heat in a desert can also get old.

The Plot

Playing games won't last,
Especially when the ghost of Christmas present meets the ghost of
Christmas past.
I tell you that when the plot thickens,
It will outwrite Charles Dickens.
It will remove every trick up your sleeve,
Way before Christmas Eve.
Victims of a player's ruse
Will be even bitterer than Scrooge.
Some people play games a lot,
But no game will usurp God's plot.

Note: Despite the references to Charles Dickens's *A Christmas Carol*,
this was inspired by an episode of *Grey's Anatomy* that originally aired
May 1, 2014.

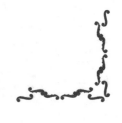

Cream of the Crop

I worked hard to get to the top,
And I wouldn't quit until I became the cream of the crop.
My ego made me brash,
And then came the big crash.

Whenever you reach the top of the slope,
Hold on tighter to the rope.
The things that go up really tend to go down,
And without the LORD God, you will drown.

Trading Up

I will never forget the words of the breakup letter
When my love left because there was someone "better."
But there's a price to pay for the sin
Of opening your relationship to let someone else in.
It may cause a world of hurt
To open the floodgates with a little flirt.
You used to say no other love would do,
Until you let someone else get close to you.
You used to say our love was heavenly,
Until you traded up for someone seemingly better than me.

Grounded

Jezebel rose and then she fell.

She probably went straight through the gates of hell.

She used to sit on several thrones,

Until she was reduced to a pile of bones.

She was trampled into the ground,

And most of her could not be found.

It's a reminder that evil ways

Will have a brutal end to their numbered days.

Living the Dream

When things are not how they seemed
Nightmares are lived, despite what was dreamed.

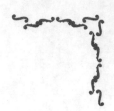
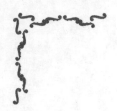

Mattered

Love no longer mattered
When the one you love left you battered.
Love is not a one-way street.
It's an intersection, where two hearts meet.

You can't remove the petals from a rose
And then wonder why it no longer grows and glows.
You'll look at the rose and no longer be able to tell,
Because when you removed the petals, it also lost its sweet smell.

Before you hit, degrade, or shout,
Place yourself in a loving timeout.
Love is a very precious gift from above.
And you never … never … never … hurt the one you love.

Seize the Power

Sometimes for the save
You have to do something extremely brave.
Some people get a feeling of power
By playing on your fears so you can cower.
But there are two sides of a pulley,
And it's no fun being victimized, even when the victim was once a
bully.

Praises

His friends treated him with disdain,
But I understand, because I can feel Job's pain.
It's easy to say that God is great
When you're not suffering my fate.
But despite everything I'm going through,
I can say the same thing too.
I still give God praise,
Despite the misery of my days.

Insert Here

Open mouth and insert foot.
What you just said wasn't well put.
I won't cut you any slack,
Because what you said can't be taken back.

Patience

If it's the last thing that I do,
I'm going to see this thing through.
I don't need the delivery date
To patiently or impatiently wait.
I have to remain in one accord,
With the divine Words of the Lord.

So if it's the very last thing that I do,
I'm going to see this thing all the way through.
Even if it's before I take my second-to-last breath,
I know God will deliver before my death.

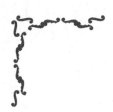

Passion

I live my life in a certain fashion.
I do things with intense passion.
I have no problems expressing the love I feel,
Because my actions are filled with zeal.

It's never enough to simply like someone a lot;
I want to love with everything I've got.
I'm not a snack for you to dabble and taste.
I have too much to give yet nothing to waste.

Plaster

Building a retaining wall with cheap plaster
Is a recipe for a big disaster.

Burnt

Life is a mountain filled with valleys and ridges.
And it's harder to traverse if you burn all the bridges.

Memories Abound

Some memories will get lost, and some will be found.
Your memories have been there for as long as you've been around.
There are memories from being awake, and when your sleep is sound;
Even during a famine, memories abound.

There are memories that make you laugh, and others make you weep.
Some memories will even visit you in your sleep.
There are memories that you discard and bury deep in the ground.
But those memories end up on the next corner that you'll go around.

Memories are pieces of your history that evoke a certain feel,
And a precious memory is more filling than a meal.
Memories will come, and memories will go,
But you'll create your next memory from the seed that you sow.

Distracted

The things that I missed, I am now reminded,
Were distractions that caused me to get blindsided.
The wrong things to which I was attracted
Were simply ploys to keep me distracted.
I thought once, but I should've thought thrice,
Because every distraction came with a severe price.

Without You

One of life's most incredible facts
Is that we can always recover from "unspeakable" acts.
We have to remove the cloak of guilt and shame
And speak the unspeakable, because adding light to darkness never
leaves it the same.
Whether from emotional or physical violence,
No one should ever suffer in silence.
The painful memories can leave us feeling broken,
Especially when they are suppressed and left unspoken.
But I, I refuse to live in misery
Because of what was done to me.
I now know I wasn't to blame.
I'm now a survivor, but what's your name?
You tried to make me feel like a lowly mushroom,
But now I'm a sweet-smelling rose in full bloom.

You made me view the world as a cold, dark place,
Until I felt the LORD God touch my face.
My pain lasted just a bit longer,
But with that touch, the Lord made me stronger.
People question my faith after what I went through,
But Jesus said we would have troubles that He'd pull us through.
Troubles test and build our resilience,
Even if they temporarily erode our confidence.
So taking things one day and step at a time is a must.
I give it to You freely, but everyone else must earn my trust.

I refuse to live a life filled with misery,

So I'm making You, my Lord, the source of my recovery.

The thing that was meant to drive us apart

Actually gave our deeper relationship a jumpstart.

My recovery wasn't a walk in the park.

But it got easier when I realized that some things only thrive in the dark.

Despite everything that I've been through,

I know I wouldn't have made it … I wouldn't have made it without You.

About the Author

The LORD God called Kollin L. Taylor to "minister to the people."
He is the author of more than thirty books that are meant to provide
edification, exhortation, and comfort for the glorification of God,
especially to the brokenhearted and those who have drifted away
from the Lord.

Kollin's published works:
Exposed Part I: The Prelude
Exposed Part II: Romantic Relationships
Exposed Part III: Vida
Exposed Part IV: The Journey Continues
Metamorphosis: The New Me
The Phenom: From My Soul
Resilience: Bend, Don't Break
The Aftermath: When the Smoke Clears and the Dust Settles
Perspective: A New Point of View
The Anatomy of a Heartbreak: When SAMson Met Delilah (narrative)
Round 2: The Battle Continues
Round 3: Still Fighting
Cool Breeze: Irie Man
Finding Joy in You: The Gift of Eternal Life

Minister to the People: Answering His Calling
The Path to Enlightenment
Knowledge Is Power: Before You Do What You're Told, Know What You're Being Told
Soul Food: Thanks, Lord, for My Daily Bread
Closet Christian: If You Deny Him, He Will Deny You
Australia: A Journey Down Under
Wrongfully Accused: When Innocence Is Not Enough
The Sidelines: Those Who Can …
Flirting with Disaster
The Sound of a Fallen Tree
Survival
Humble Pie: A Gift from God
Second Chances: Worthy of Redemption
God's Kitchen: His Slow Cooked Stew
On Trial: A Test of My Faith
God Speaks to My Soul
God, the Love of My Life
Labor Pains: Waiting to Push!

Author photo by Sterlin King

Connect with the author
Facebook: https://www.facebook.com/KollinLTaylor
Twitter: @KollinLTaylor